The Truck Is Stuck

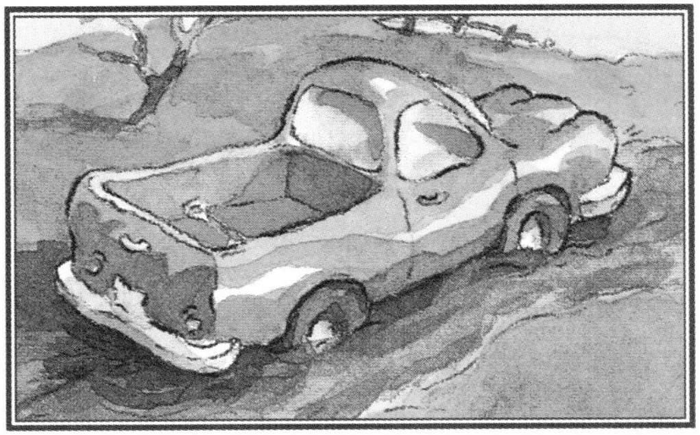

Written by Claire Daniel
Illustrated by Abby Carter

Oh, no!

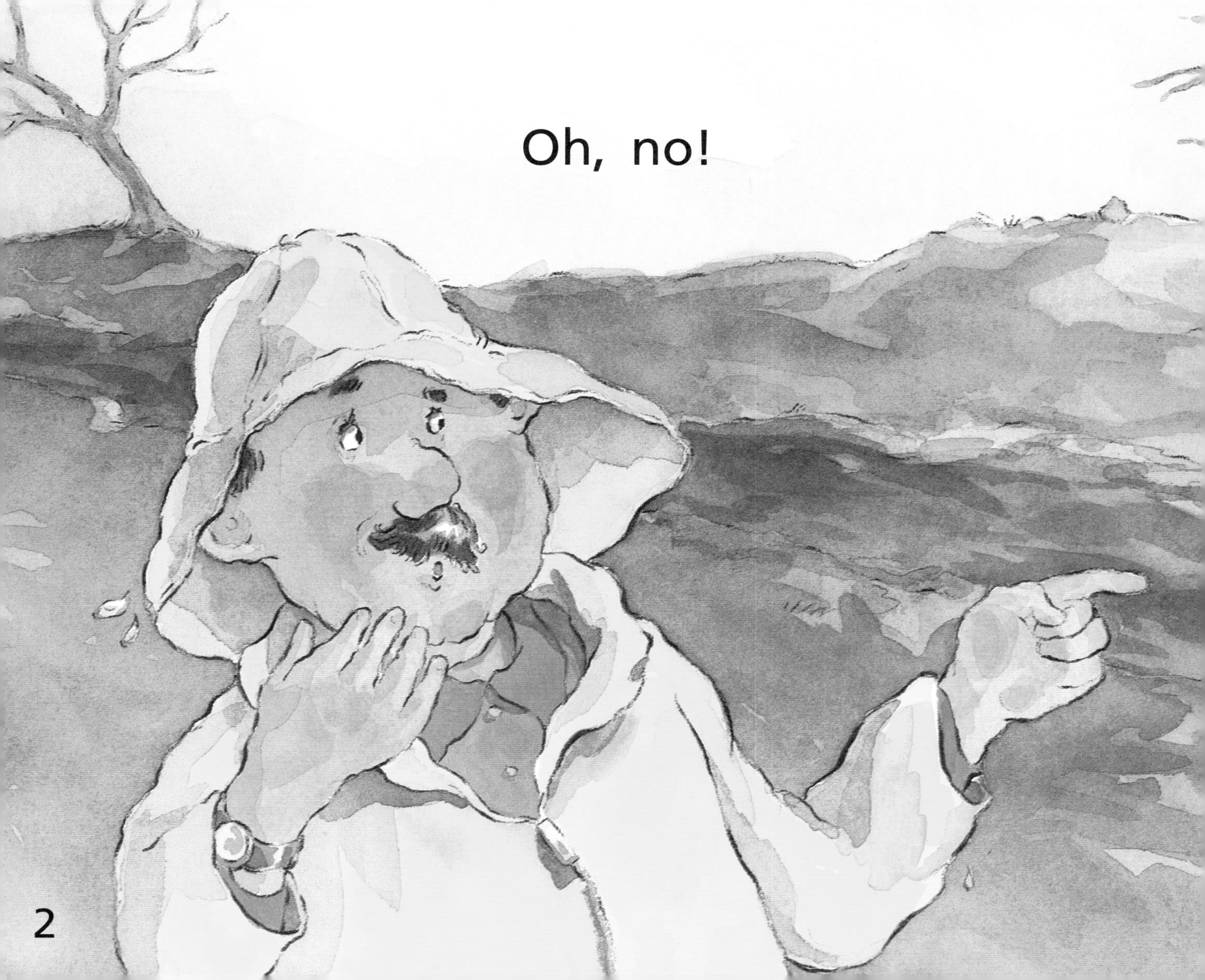

The truck is stuck.

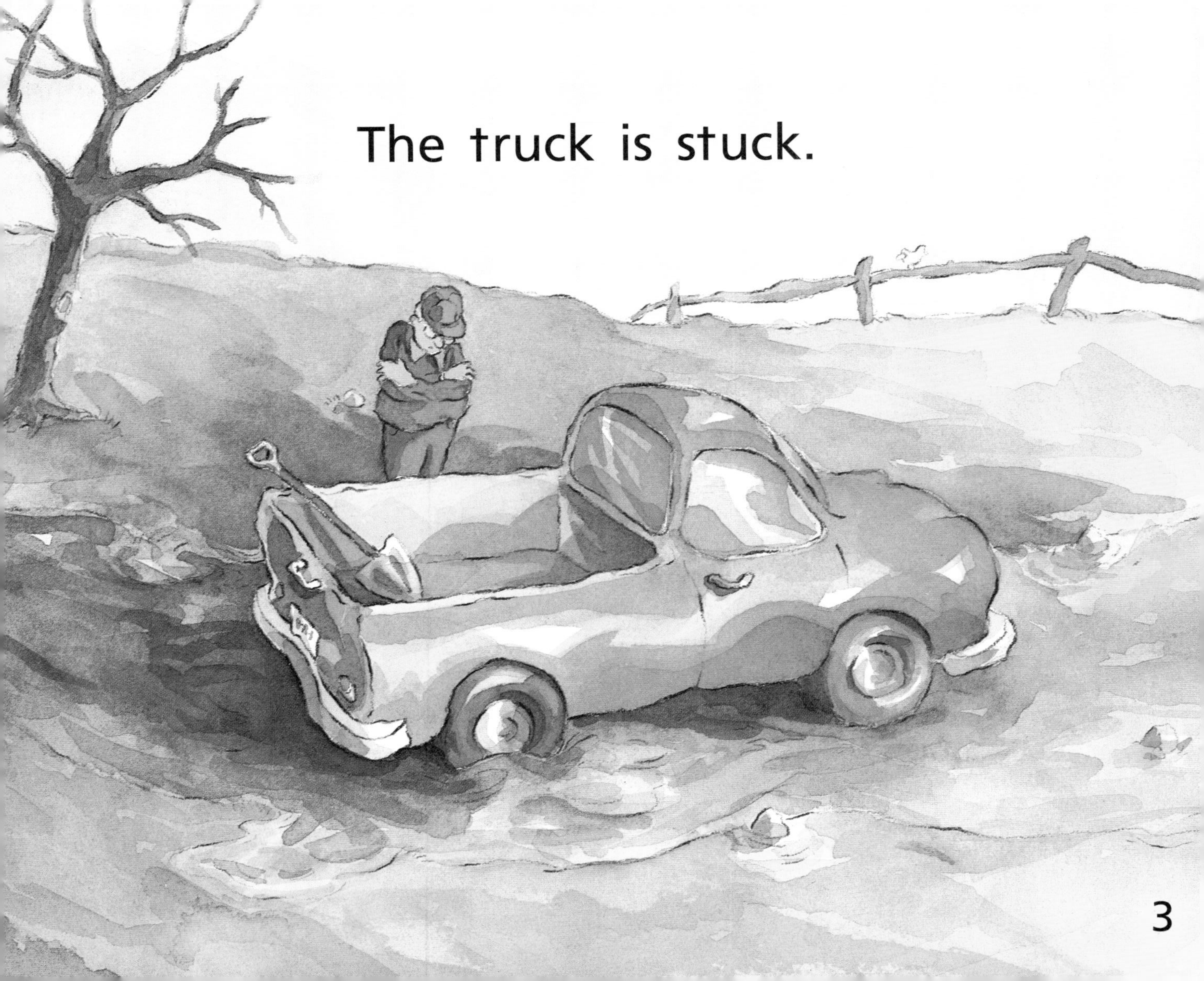

Oh, no!

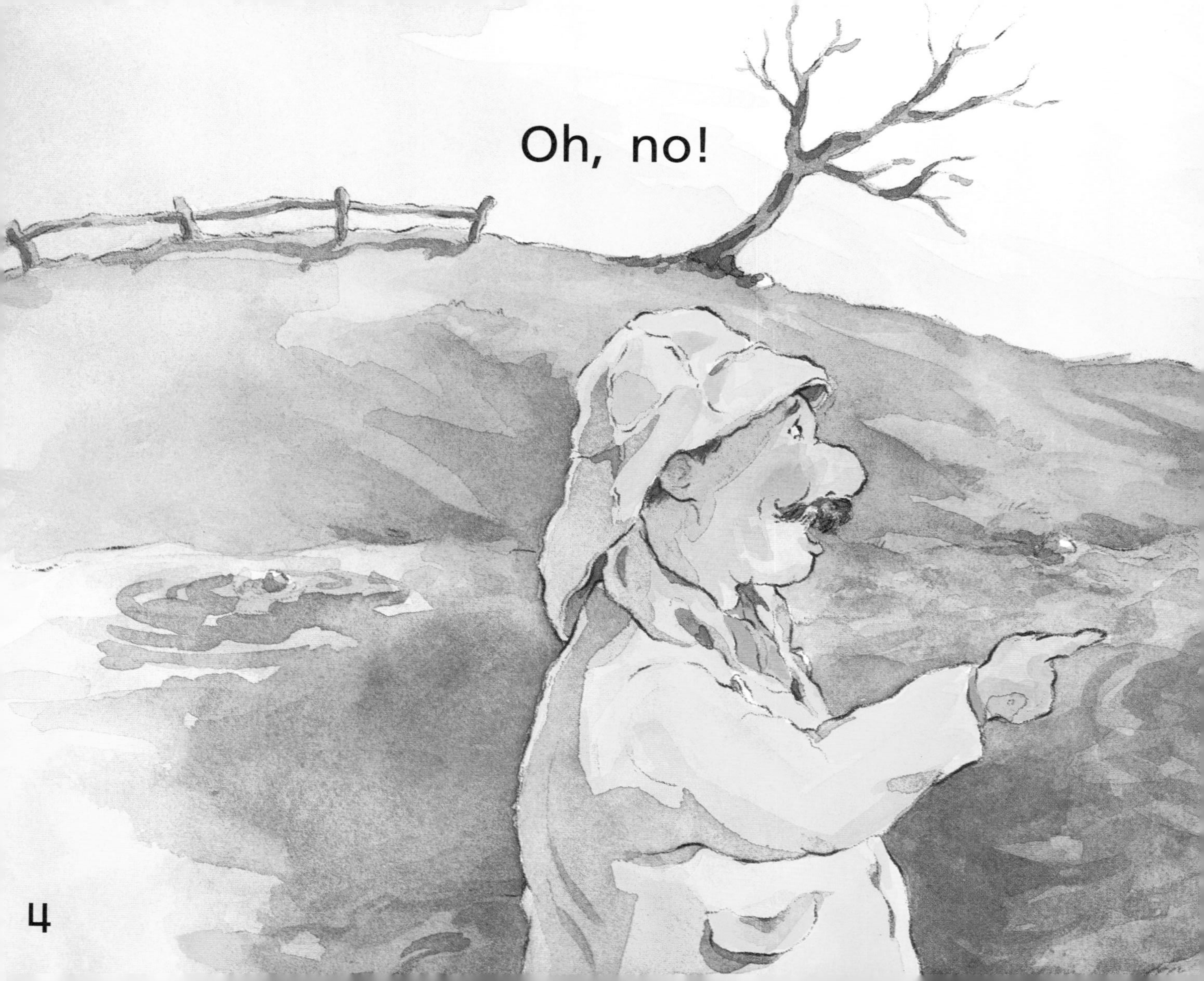

The bus is stuck.

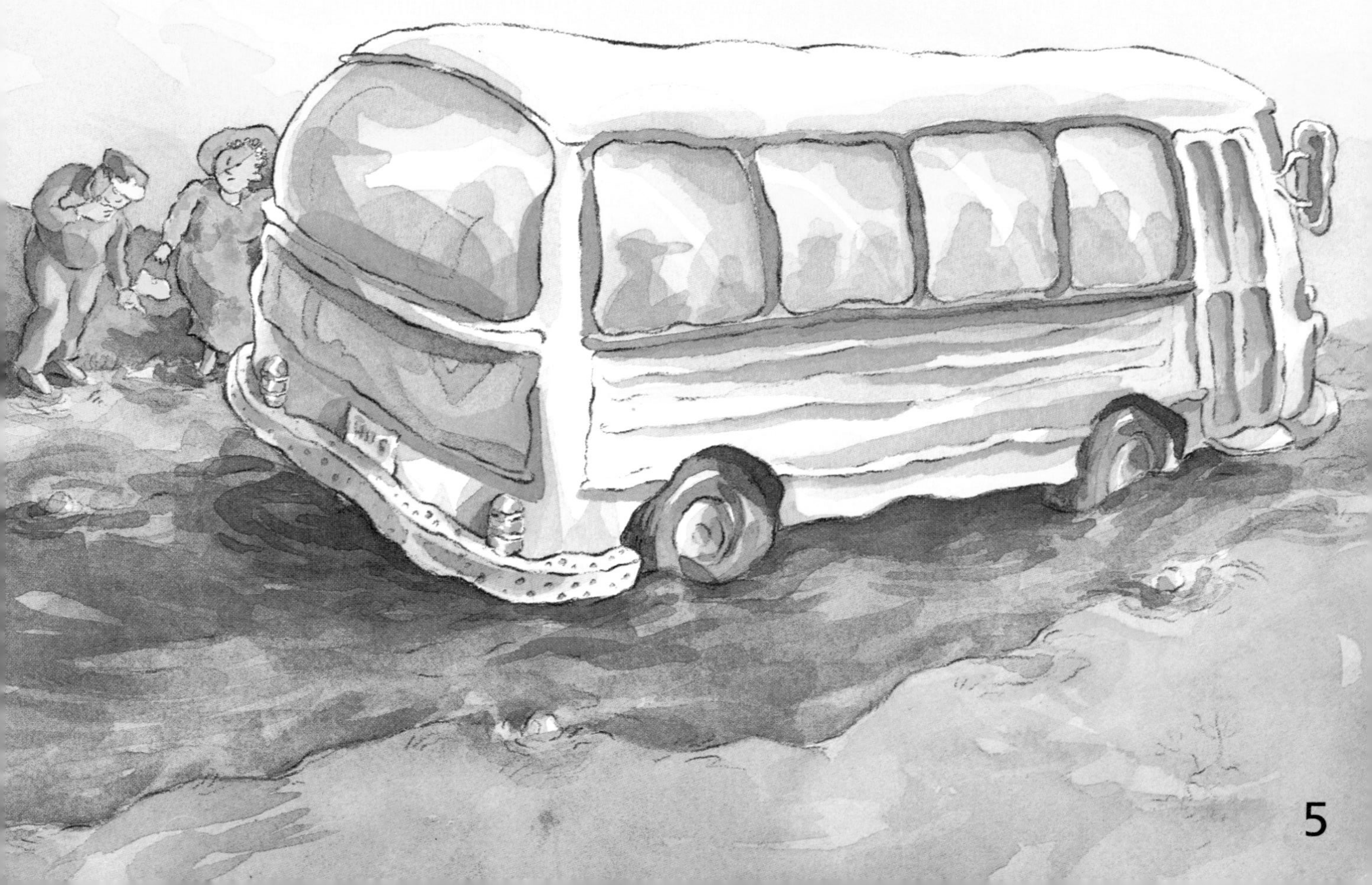

Oh, no!

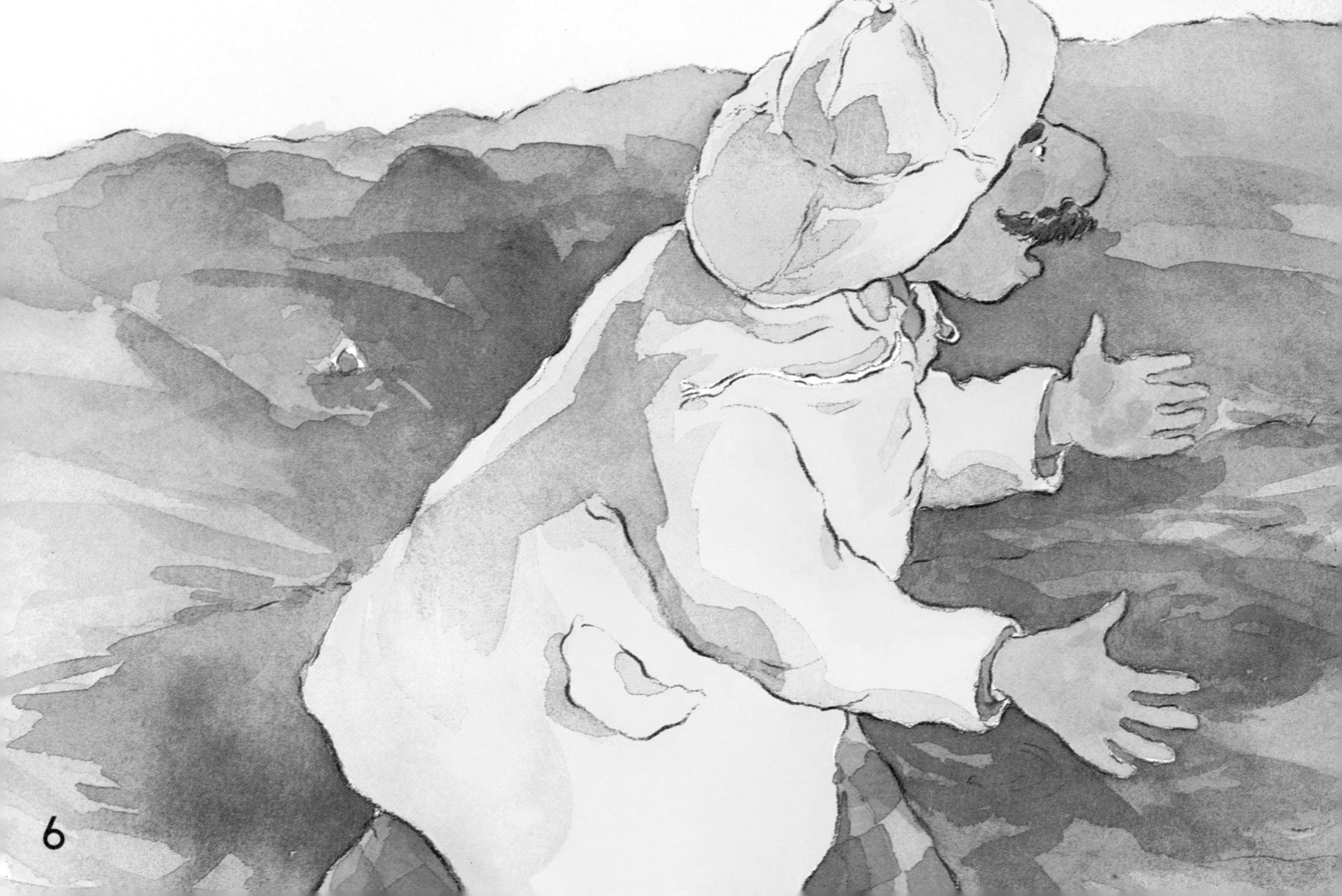

The car is stuck.

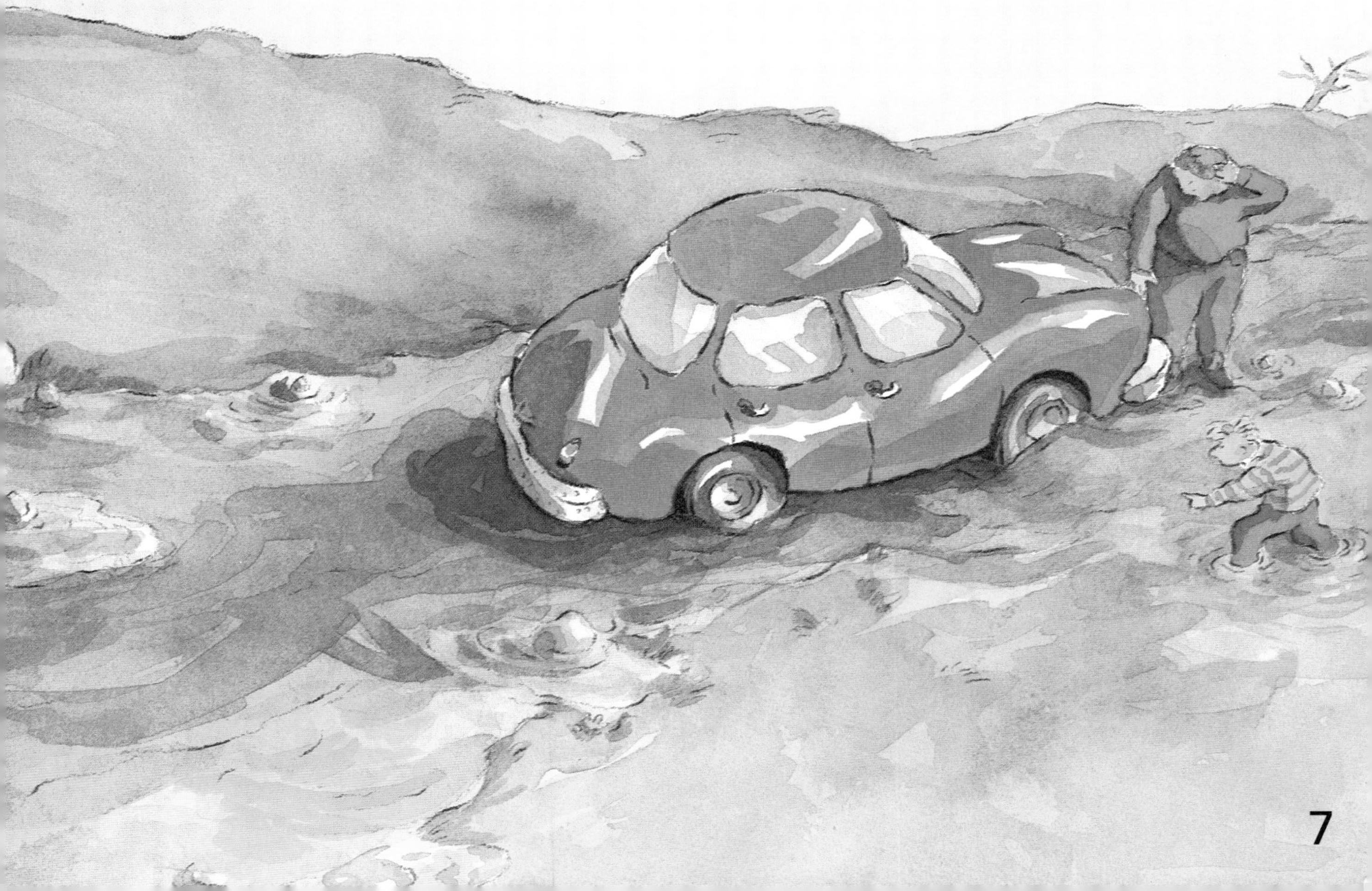

Oh, no! I am stuck!

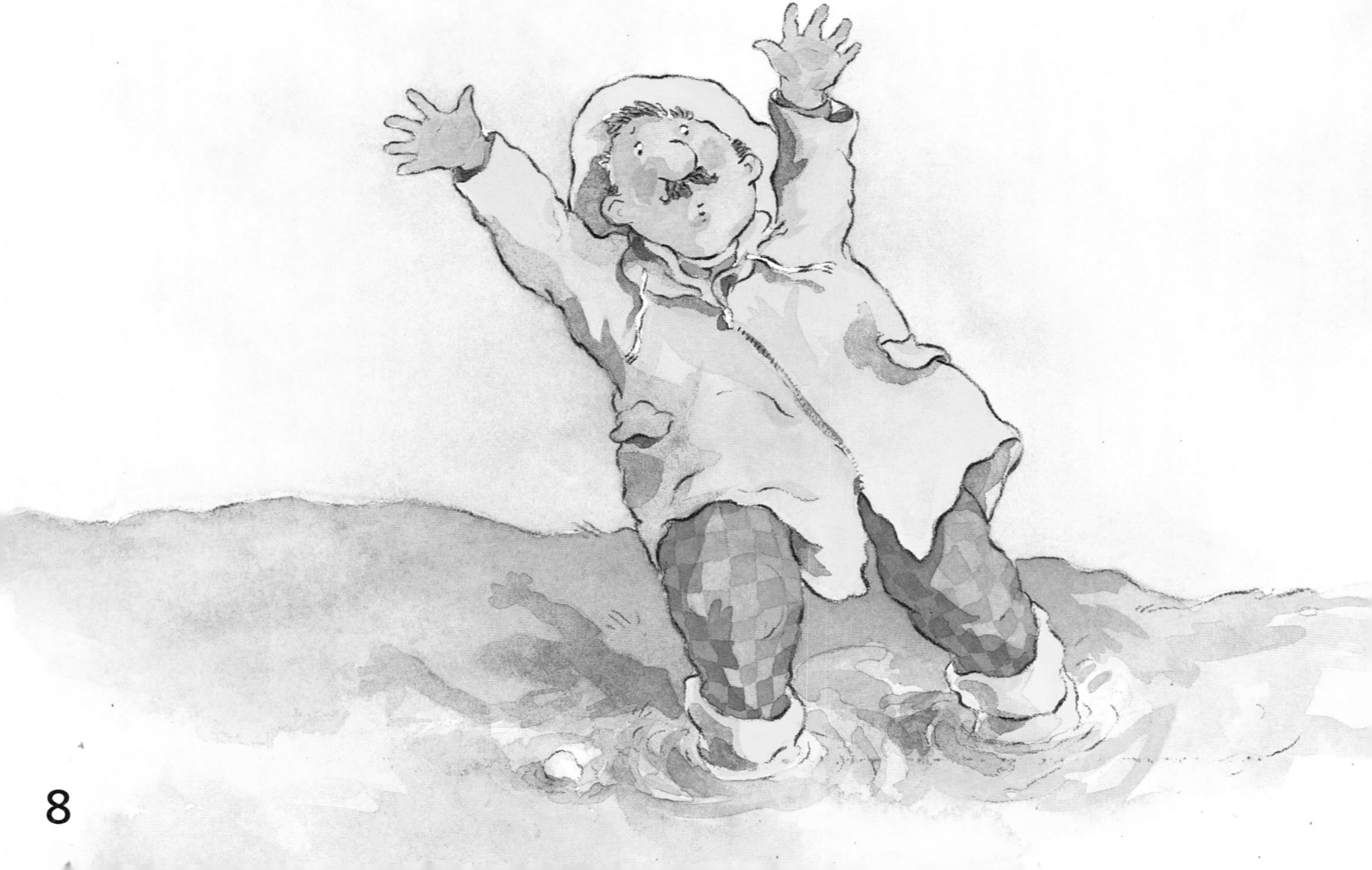